Paws for Reflection

50 DEVOS

— for —

CAT MOMS

DaySpring

LIVE YOUR FAITH

Paws for Reflection: 50 Devos for Cat Moms
Copyright © 2021 by DaySpring Cards, Inc.
First Edition, July 2021

Published by:

21154 Highway 16 East
Siloam Springs, AR 72761
dayspring.com

Written by: Janice Thompson
Cover Design by: Becca Barnett

Printed in China
Prime: J4964
ISBN: 978-1-64454-983-4

Contents

Our Four-Legged Friends

Whether they're snoozing in the afternoon sunlight or winding themselves around our ankles, cats are a lovely addition to our lives. They latch on to our hearts and won't let go.

If you've had the joy of knowing and loving a cat, then you already know what a blessing that precious companionship can be. They walk with us through the lowest valleys and curl up in our laps when we're needing a friend. With their purring, rubbing, mews, and constant affection, they fill a void that humans couldn't possibly fill.

These precious creatures show us affection through their eyes, their tails, and even their head-butting. And though they may encroach upon our personal space, we love them anyway. Cats draw us closer to our Creator, the very One who placed that sense of faithfulness inside of them.

In the pages of this book, you will find several light-hearted cat tails (er, tales), to remind you of God's abiding presence. Like that precious little kitty, your heavenly Father never plans to leave you or forsake you. May you be reminded that He's with you, no matter what you're going through.

A Higher Purr-spective

Set your minds on things above, not on earthly things.

COLOSSIANS 3:2 NIV

• • •

Precious, a beautiful two-year-old tabby, loved her new scratch tower. After s-t-r-e-t-c-h-i-n-g and scratching to her heart's content, she would leap onto the highest platform, scratch a few more times, and then settle down for a long nap.

Many times, Mandy, her owner, would look up to discover her beloved feline wasn't sleeping at all. Instead, Precious kept a watchful eye on the goings-on below. The observant kitty watched as the kids arrived home from school, arms loaded with books. She remained still on her perch as the family enjoyed their evening meal and even watched over them as they gathered around the coffee table to play a board game.

Apparently, Precious loved her perspective from on high, for she stayed up there for hours on end, only coming down at mealtime. Then she would start the process all over again, stretching, scratching, and heading up, up, up so that she could maintain her point of view. Sometimes she would even spend the whole night sleeping there.

When it comes to how we view life, we have a lot to learn from Precious. Many times, we trudge through a fog of uncomfortable circumstances, seeing them only from our own earthly point of view. We forget to ask God for His perspective. If we took the time to do that, perhaps we would see that things are a bit different from His point of view. Maybe we would realize that God is up to more than we imagined, teaching us lessons from the valleys we're walking through. A higher perspective might also give us a godly filter through which we could view relationships. Perhaps we could begin to see others as the Lord sees them, if only we could catch a glimpse from on high.

It's time to make a leap onto that perch, sweet woman of God! Oh, the things you'll see!

Lord, thank You for giving me
Your perspective. It helps to know
there are greater plans at work.

AMEN.

2

Nose Blind

If we confess our sins, he is faithful and just to forgive us our sins and to cleanse us from all unrighteousness.

I JOHN 1:9 ESV

• • •

Denise kept the family cat's litter box in her son's bathroom, far away from her own part of the house. She gave fourteen-year-old Josh the task of cleaning out the box every three days. He reluctantly agreed. She purchased expensive kitty litter and put the bag in the bathroom cupboard so it would be handy. She also provided him with a small shovel and trash bags so he would have no excuses. But would he follow through?

For a while, everything seemed fine. Then one day she walked into his bathroom to put some towels away and was knocked backward by the smell. A quick glance down revealed the truth: the litter box hadn't been cleaned out in ages. Whew! Talk about a stench! Worse yet, the bag of kitty litter sat nearby, unopened. She could hardly believe her eyes or her nose.

Denise called her son into the bathroom and gave him a stern talking-to about the situation. He looked a little confused as she went on and on about the odor.

"What odor?" Josh asked. "I don't smell anything."

"Seriously?" she responded.

"Yeah." He leaned over the litter box and sniffed, then shrugged.

Aha. Apparently, days of living with the smell had caused him to become nose blind.

The same thing can happen in our spiritual lives, if we're not paying attention. Bad choices become habitual, then shift into a lifestyle we seek to justify. After a while, we no longer see our choices as bad. We've made excuses for so long that we've become nose blind to them.

Maybe it's time for a reality check! Today, ask God if you need to take inventory of the areas of your life that need adjustment. Is there something you need to toss? If so, clean out that proverbial litter box, once and for all. You'll be so happy to breathe freely again.

Dear Lord, I'm sorry for the
wrong choices I've made. May I
never grow blind to them, I pray.

AMEN.

3

Licking Old Wounds

*No, Christian brothers, I do not have that life yet.
But I do one thing. I forget everything that is behind
me and look forward to that which is ahead of me.
My eyes are on the crown. I want to win the race and get
the crown of God's call from heaven through Christ Jesus.*

PHILIPPIANS 3:13–14 NLV

• • •

Madeline worried about her cat, Oscar. He had—for lack of a better term—licking problems. From the moment he woke up until he went to bed at night, the anxious feline cleaned himself. Over and over his tongue lapped at his fur until he coughed up hair balls, one after the other. Only when he dozed off in the late-morning sunlight would the repetitive motions come to a halt. Then, as soon as he awoke, he started all over again.

Frustrated with his never-ending obsession, Madeline finally took him to the vet, who explained that some cats self-soothe by cleaning themselves. He gave her some ideas for how she could distract Oscar and fill his day with more meaningful activities. So Madeline spent more time petting him and offered him toys to play with. Before long, his licking slowed.

We're not much different than Oscar. If we're not

careful, we can waste our precious hours licking old wounds. We rehearse the words that were spoken over us. We can't stop thinking about the pain of betrayal. We fret over broken relationships. We replay those situations over and over in our minds and hearts and try to figure out what we could have done differently.

God wants to divert us, to give us better ways to fill our days. He longs for us to come to Him, to offer Him the things that are hard to let go. Then He's happy to distract us with plenty of affection and love, along with newer, fresher relationships and total healing.

What are you holding on to today, precious woman of God? Perhaps it's time to open those hands and let it go. After all, you've already licked that problem.

Lord, thank You for the reminder
that I don't need to nurse old
wounds. I need to trust in Your healing,
Father, that I might be set free.

AMEN.

Home Is Where the Cat Is

For He chose us in Him before the creation of the world to be holy and blameless in His sight. In love He predestined us for adoption to sonship through Jesus Christ, in accordance with His pleasure and will—to the praise of His glorious grace, which He has freely given us in the One He loves.

EPHESIANS 1:4–6 NIV

• • •

Janie looked up from the sink full of dirty dishes as her two preteen daughters ran into the room.

"Mom! Guess what?" Eliza was bouncing up and down. "There's a white cat—"

"In our tree," Adeline jumped in. "It's beautiful. Can we keep it?"

"I'm sure it has a home," Janie said as she reached for the cloth to dry her hands. "But I'll come take a look."

She followed the girls out to the front yard. They pointed to a gorgeous white cat, high in the branches. Using some of their dog's canned food, Janie managed to coax the kitty down. She couldn't believe how sweet and tiny the frail thing was, in desperate need of food. And so affectionate! The precious kitty couldn't get enough cuddles and kisses.

A local vet found no microchip. With no collar or tag, no owner could be traced. Still, Janie tried. Over the next several days, she put up signs with the cat's picture and posted in her neighborhood social media group to try to find the owner. No one came forward. Good thing, since Eliza and Adeline were getting attached. For that matter, Janie was too. At the end of the second week, they made it official. They gave the kitty a permanent name—Snowball—and a permanent home.

Pet adoption is a wonderful thing. It gives the animal a new lease on life with protection, food, water, shelter, and lots of love. Sound familiar? The same is true when God adopts us into His family. We once were lost (in sin and selfishness). But when we come to know His Son, Jesus, as Savior, He sweeps us into the fold, calls us His children, and provides all we need to not only survive but thrive!

How wonderful to be adopted by the King of kings!

Lord, I'm so grateful You adopted me. You rescued me—not from a tree but from myself. You coaxed me down with Your love and swept me into the family. How grateful I am!

AMEN.

Purr-ty Is as Purr-ty Does

And whatever you do, whether in word or deed,
do it all in the name of the Lord Jesus,
giving thanks to God the Father through Him.

COLOSSIANS 3:17 NIV

• • •

"Susan, that's the prettiest cat I've ever seen!" Mandy said as she observed her friend's gorgeous tabby cat, Milo. "Such lovely coloring. And I've never seen such piercing blue eyes. Wow! You're so lucky to have such a beautiful pet."

Susan beamed with pride. "Thanks. We think he's handsome too."

"He certainly is." Mandy instinctively reached over to stroke the gorgeous feline, but the cat startled her by lashing out at her and leaving scratch marks on her hand.

Shocked and horrified, Mandy pulled her hand back. She glanced down at the bloody marks, now trembling. "Whoa. Never saw that coming."

"Mandy, I'm so sorry!" Susan scooped up the cat and cradled him in her arms. "That happens sometimes. He's a bit naughty."

Naughty might be a bit of an understatement. This cat was a danger to others. So much for focusing on his gorgeous exterior when he had an attitude like that.

Mama wasn't kidding when she used the words "Pretty is as pretty does." It's pointless to worry about external beauty when you're mean and cranky on the inside. People might see the dressed-up version of you, but when the goo in the middle comes oozing out, they see a whole different side, one that might send them running for the hills!

God wants His girls to be gorgeous, but He cares far more about the inside. Making yourself internally beautiful starts by submitting your will to His. If you're struggling with anger or irritability, ask Him to tackle that for you. He's more than happy to do so. Trust Him to make the necessary changes in your heart so that you truly are beautiful inside and out.

Lord, I'll admit, I often dress up the outside but forget to fix who I am inside. I've got issues that sometimes bubble up to the surface. Unfortunately, those I love are most often the ones who see it firsthand. Today I give my insides to You. Make them beautiful, as only You can, Father.

AMEN.

6

An Adventurous Spirit

Where shall I go from your Spirit? Or where shall I flee from your presence? If I ascend to heaven, you are there! If I make my bed in Sheol, you are there! If I take the wings of the morning and dwell in the uttermost parts of the sea, even there your hand shall lead me, and your right hand shall hold me.

PSALM 139:7–10 ESV

• • •

Rocky, a seven-year-old tomcat, had a great home. He lived with Bob and Susan in a nice house out in the country. But he preferred the great outdoors, and in the area where they lived, outdoor cats were A-okay. This was great news for Rocky, who loved nothing more than to roam.

On occasion, Rocky would take his roaming to a whole new level. He would disappear for a couple of days, leaving his owners wondering where he'd gone.

Oh, but the adventures he had! He discovered a creek on the edge of the property, one with still waters, where the afternoon sunlight reflected in glorious rays. He figured out the neighbor's system of feeding the dog on the front porch at eight every morning and helped himself before the pooch showed up. He even did a little digging in the neighbor's garden, just for fun, pulling up some lovely daffodils and nibbling on some calla lilies.

Rocky would eventually return home, but things at the family property didn't seem as exciting now that he'd experienced the outside world. He'd stay put for some food and a good night's sleep, then head out once again, ready for another adventure.

Rocky's adventurous life sounds appealing, doesn't it? Sometimes we get so comfortable in our daily routines, so at ease with our self-imposed boundary lines, that we forget to be adventurous! Perhaps God is calling you to something big, something brave. Like Rocky, you will have to step outside of your comfort zone and explore the possibilities. There's a great big world waiting out there, and the Lord has big things for you to accomplish!

Lord, I'm ready to step out of my comfort zone and live an adventurous life! Lead me to places yet unseen, that I might do great exploits for You!

AMEN.

7

The Cat's Meow

Do all things without grumbling or disputing.

PHILIPPIANS 2:14 ESV

• • •

When Caroline adopted the tiny white kitten with the cute black button nose, she named her Sweet Thang. It just seemed to fit the adorable little feline.

Things went well with the kitten until Caroline's employer told her she could work from home. Each morning she would sit at her desk and attempt to get in the right frame of mind to work. But the ornery feline would make it impossible. Sweet Thang would meow incessantly, never letting up until Caroline allowed her to sit on her lap. Only one problem—typing with a cat on your lap isn't comfortable. Or realistic.

Caroline found herself making mistakes and losing her ability to focus. So, down the cat would go. Then, the meowing would begin again in earnest until Caroline relented once again. Sweet Thang would get her way, but the price Caroline paid was high, since it greatly affected her work.

Cats can be clingy at times. It's great that they're so loving, but the never-ending meowing if they don't get their way can be aggravating, especially if it affects your work. Sometimes the only thing you can do is separate yourself from your furry friend so that you can have the peace of mind necessary to get the job done.

In some ways, we're a little like Sweet Thang. We demand our own way. We want what we want when we want it. And we complain and whine until we get it. Oh c'mon! You know it's true! We're all guilty of it sometimes. If we are raised by parents who give in at every little "Meow!" we can grow into demanding adults who often can't see past themselves to the needs of others. (Maybe you know a few people like that!)

Maybe it's time to stop meowing. Ask God to shift your focus from your own wants and wishes to the needs of others. He'll do it, if only you ask. And you just might be surprised to find He will give you peace along the way.

Father, I'll admit that I've demanded my own way at times. I've probably irritated others with my whining. Help me overcome this selfish tendency, I pray.

AMEN.

8

Self-Cleaning

*Now may the God of peace himself sanctify you completely,
and may your whole spirit and soul and body be kept
blameless at the coming of our Lord Jesus Christ.*

I THESSALONIANS 5:23 ESV

. . .

If you're a cat owner, you've probably already figured out that most felines aren't crazy about water. Try to bathe a cat, and . . . watch out! They're liable to scratch your eyes out or take off flying across the room!

Thank goodness cats come with a built-in self-washing system. They love to bathe themselves, and their rough tongues make the process easy. With it, they can scrape away mud, dust, crumbs, and other debris. Felines are pretty flexible too! They can reach places on their own bodies you wouldn't imagine. So they don't mind this task at all.

Watching a cat bathe himself serves as a good reminder that we need to be self-cleaning too. When we make messes, we've got to be willing to clean up after ourselves. Sometimes it can seem overwhelming. (Think of your kitchen after Thanksgiving dinner.) It's a dirty job, but someone's gotta do it, girl!

Now think about other messes you've made—the

friendships you've destroyed with harsh words, the mistakes you made on the job, the times you should have done something but didn't. Someone's got to clean up those messes too. And the very best person for the job is you.

It's not fun to clean up after yourself, but think of how good you'll feel when things are fresh and new again. And you'll be honoring God with your obedience as well.

Lord, with Your help, I'll clean up my messes. For the times I've let things get too out of hand, I'm sorry. Clean and tidy is the way to go, so I'll do my best next time.

AMEN.

CATS ARE CONNOISSEURS OF COMFORT.

James Herriot

9

Rewriting the Story

For I know the plans I have for you,
declares the LORD, plans for welfare and not
for evil, to give you a future and a hope.

JEREMIAH 29:11 ESV

• • •

Hannah worked from home as a novelist. She loved to craft stories. The busy young woman sat for hours at her computer with her cat, Tiny, at her feet. The little feline seemed content to pass the hours peacefully, as long as Hannah didn't move from her spot.

One afternoon Hannah took a break from her writing. She started down the stairs to grab a snack and was surprised Tiny hadn't followed.

"Tiny?" she called out. "Where are you, girl?"

The little cat came bounding down the stairs and wound herself around Hannah's ankles, purring contentedly.

A few minutes later Hannah went back upstairs. She touched the keyboard on her computer and the screen lit up, revealing the oddest-looking assortment of jumbled letters and numbers in the middle of her story. Where her last (sensible) paragraph left off, chaos began.

As if to prove a point, Tiny jumped up onto the desk and stepped directly onto the keyboard, creating even more mess.

"Ah. I see what you did there." Hannah put the cat down on the ground and deleted all the jumbled text from her document.

Sometimes life feels a bit like Tiny's addition to the story. We're going along just fine, getting our own way, writing our own story . . . and then something interrupts the flow. In an instant, before we can cry out, "What's going on here?" we're faced with calamities we never saw coming. Total chaos ensues as this random force takes over. The death of a loved one. A financial catastrophe. A health struggle. These aren't the things we'd hoped to see in our life story, but there they are.

Don't you wish life had a delete key so that you could eliminate the overwhelming parts? During these seasons of interruption, trusting God becomes so important. We come to realize the story was never ours to begin with. He was always the One with the pen in hand, crafting the tale. He loves us and wants to work everything for our good, which means we can trust Him . . . even when the story goes astray.

I trust You, even now, Lord.
Take the pen and write my story.

AMEN.

- 27 -

Rescued!

But God demonstrates His own love for us in this:
While we were still sinners, Christ died for us.

ROMANS 5:8 NIV

• • •

Thousands of people looked on via the Internet as Mercy worked to save a tiny kitten who'd fallen into a small pipe and was now lodged fifty feet below ground. In all her years of animal rescue, she'd never had a case like this. She managed to lower her camera down by a rope and could see the little kitty in obvious distress, tightly wedged. She could also see that the pipe kept going. If they didn't find an answer to this problem—and soon— he might continue to fall down even farther.

It took a team of helpers to devise a plan to lower a tool with a loop to curl under the kitten and pull it up, but the process proved long and agonizing. Many times, they would try and fail. Turned out, the tool didn't quite reach, so it had to be lengthened.

She could hear the little kitten's pitiful cries and wondered if he—or she—would make it. Hours went by before the little one was finally safe above ground. Celebratory praise broke out, and Mercy found herself crying as she held the helpless kitten close. What joy, to rescue one so fragile!

If we get that emotional rescuing animals, can you even imagine how God must feel when one of His children returns to the fold? Jesus gave His very life to rescue us. When we find ourselves trapped, as that precious kitten did, He will go to any lengths to woo us back to Him. And oh, the joy He feels once He sweeps us into His arms. Just like that celebratory response from the crowd, all of heaven throws a party when God rescues us from our pain and worry. What a joy, to be held in the arms of an almighty King who longs to give us a safe place to land when life gets scary.

Father, in case I haven't said it enough, thank You for rescuing me! I'm so grateful You swept in to save me.

AMEN.

11

Space Invaders

Love is patient, love is kind. It does not envy,
it does not boast, it is not proud. It does not
dishonor others, it is not self-seeking, it is not easily
angered, it keeps no record of wrongs.

I CORINTHIANS 13:4–5 NIV

. . .

"Sheba, move over and let me sit down." Brittany waved her arms, as if expecting the ornery cat to give up her space on the sofa. Sheba refused to move.

Brittany gave her a tiny nudge and the feline eventually moved over, though slightly. Brittany settled into her spot on the sofa and reached for her laptop, ready to get to work on a project that was overdue. Unfortunately, Sheba saw the open laptop as an opportunity to nuzzle even closer. She tried to wedge herself under Brittany's arm, which made typing impossible.

"Really, Sheba?" Brittany picked the cat up and moved her over.

This lasted about ten seconds. Then Sheba jumped onto the back of the sofa, eased her way in Brittany's direction, and ended up wrapped around the back of Brittany's neck. Finally ready to give up, Brittany rose, put the cat outside the room, and closed the door.

Maybe you've got a space invader like Sheba, someone who hovers a bit too close. Or maybe you've become one to a friend or loved one. It's one thing to care; it's another to hover like a helicopter.

Space invaders can get on our nerves. They're in our business when they shouldn't be. It's uncomfortable. But it's equally uncomfortable for others when we act like that.

Have you invaded anyone's space lately? Are you hovering over a child, a spouse, or a friend? If you're too tightly wrapped around their proverbial necks, your loved ones might be feeling a bit suffocated right now. Maybe it's time to step back and give that person some space. Sure, he (or she) might stumble and fall. But maybe it's time to let God pick them up instead of you.

Lord, I don't want to be a helicopter mom (or spouse ... or friend). Show me how to let go of the reins and give my loved one some much-needed space.

AMEN.

12

Practically Purr-fect in Every Way

You make known to me the path of life; You will fill me with joy in Your presence, with eternal pleasures at Your right hand.

PSALM 16:11 NIV

• • •

After her mother died, Candy went into a deep depression. She found it difficult to get out of bed in the mornings. Her energy level seemed lower than usual. Sure, she kept going to work—she had no choice. She even managed to show up to church from time to time, where she sat in her usual spot on the second-to-last row. But her zeal for life had waned, at least for now, and she couldn't seem to get it back. God seemed far away, and she wondered if she would ever feel that passion for Him again. As a result, she pulled away from the Lord, her prayer times becoming a thing of the past.

Evenings proved to be the most comforting time of day. After dinner, Candy would curl up on the sofa. Her cat, Nonny, would snuggle close, happy to be with her owner. In those moments, as Candy stroked Nonny's soft white fur, all of Candy's troubles disappeared. Her life felt practically purr-fect, in fact. Nonny didn't seem to have any troubles either, if such a thing could be judged from her purrs of contentment. She settled into a blissful state, curled up near her master and enjoying their quiet time together.

Maybe you've had that same experience—feeling like God was far away. It's time to reconnect, to sit at His feet, to curl up at His side and allow Him to give you the love and affection you need to get through this current struggle. He hasn't moved, but maybe you have. If you're not feeling close, do all you can to draw near. Do your best to long for Him again, that you might find the healing and comfort you need to get you through.

Lord, I know You've promised never to leave me or forsake me. During seasons when I feel distant, please give me a nudge in Your direction. I don't ever want to walk through the valleys without You nearby, Father.

AMEN.

Drawn to the Warmth

The islanders showed us unusual kindness. They built a fire
and welcomed us all because it was raining and cold.

ACTS 28:2 NIV

• • •

Cats love warm spaces. Lying on the back porch in the
midafternoon sunlight. Lounging on their cat tower
inside the living room window as the morning sun beams
in. Curled up in their master's lap, where body heat
comforts and calms them. Yes, any time they can move
toward the heat, they will.

Put a cat in a cold space, however, and he becomes
uncomfortable. Cranky. Ill at ease. He'll look for a warm
place to retreat, to get away from the cold.

Sometimes we're the same way, aren't we? We tend
to gravitate toward warm people. Put us in a room with
a bunch of stiff, cold people and we want to slink off to
look for someone welcoming and kind. Oh, but bump
into a warm person and we feel right at home. The
conversation comes naturally, and the kindness opens a
door to potential relationship.

God designed us to be warm toward others and
ourselves. If we put off that "Hey, you can chat with me"

vibe, people will gravitate toward us. But put off that "I'm busy; I'm cranky; I'm up to my eyeballs in bills and kids" look and people will go running in the opposite direction.

Jesus was warm. He drew His twelve disciples to His side with ease because they saw—and felt—something genuine and welcoming in Him. He stirred up possibilities within them and made them see themselves in a new way. The same will be true of you if you'll open your heart to the possibility that God wants to use you to warm this world up, one person at a time.

Lord, I love warm-hearted people!
They bring me such comfort. Erase any
cold places in my heart today, Father.
May people be drawn to me because of my
great love for them and for You.

AMEN.

Thief on the Prowl

The robber comes only to steal and to kill and to destroy.
I came so they might have life, a great full life.

JOHN 10:10 NLV

• • •

Laurie glanced at her watch. Five thirty. If she rushed, she could make it to the grocery store, pick up that one item she'd forgotten to purchase for dinner, and still make it back in time to cook the meal. She glanced at the package of ground turkey breast thawing on the counter. Another half hour and it would be ready to cook. Everything should work out perfectly.

She rushed to the store, grabbed the pasta sauce, and then raced back to the house, arriving right at six o'clock. Her cat, Ollie, wound himself around her ankles and purred. "Did you miss me, little guy?" Laurie asked. He responded by circling her feet once more.

She patted him on the head and then got to work, emptying the grocery bag. She grabbed a skillet and reached for the ground turkey breast . . . finding the package empty.

"What in the world?" Sure enough, the Styrofoam container remained intact on the counter, the plastic wrap in shreds around it, but there was no meat to be found.

"No way. Ollie!"

She hollered the cat's name and he slunk her way, as if to ask, "Yes? Did you need me?"

"Did you . . . I mean, how in the world could you . . .?" She stared at the empty meat container once more.

Animals can be little thieves when they want to be, but we need to be on the lookout for an even bigger adversary. The Bible says that the enemy comes to steal, kill, and destroy. He sneaks in when we least expect it (just like Ollie) and tries to ruin everything—our health, our relationships, even our connection and time with God.

Today, be on the lookout for the enemy's tactics. He's sneaky, that one. He's always out to convince you that you are unworthy or inadequate. He's working overtime to make you think that you are alone, that no one cares. He's purring, "You're not special. No one sees you." But you're on to him! You've learned not to fall for those tricks. You've decided not to listen to those annoying purrs, no matter how loud they get.

Lord, I'll keep my eyes wide open. I won't let the enemy of my soul steal from me any longer. Help me face him down, I pray.

AMEN

15

Friends in High Places

Out of my distress I called on the LORD;
the LORD answered me and set me free.

PSALM 118:5 ESV

. . .

Louise had heard about people calling the fire department to rescue a cat from a tree but had never experienced it personally . . . until Jade, her Siamese kitten, got stuck way up high in a pine tree. The little sixteen-week-old kitten was terrified and refused to move. She seemed to be frozen in place, and her cries were enough to alert the whole neighborhood.

Louise didn't own a ladder tall enough to reach Jade, who clung to the side of the tree and wailed. With no one else to turn to, she called the fire department. Six minutes later three burly firefighters stood in her front yard, analyzing the situation. It didn't take long to get to Jade, once they set up their ladder. Minutes later, the terrified feline curled up in her owner's arms, still shaking.

"You're lucky they came for you, little one!" Louise said as she gave Jade a scratch behind the ears. She thanked the firefighters profusely and they headed off on their way.

It's nice to have friends in high places, isn't it? They come to our rescue when we can't rescue ourselves. Think of this: Of all the people you know, the One who's the very best at rescue is your Savior, Jesus Christ. He doesn't need a ladder to get to you. There's no tree you can climb that's too high for Him, no valley you can walk through where He won't see you.

God longs to rescue you from yourself and from the calamities you find yourself in. Don't panic. Just call out to Him and then watch Him scale that tree to bring you to safety once again. Oh, what love the Father shows to those who trust Him!

Father, I've needed rescuing more than once. Thank You for sweeping in and saving me (sometimes from myself). I'm so grateful to You, my Savior!

AMEN.

Hiss-terical

Get rid of all bitterness, rage and anger, brawling
and slander, along with every form of malice.
Be kind and compassionate to one another,
forgiving each other, just as in Christ God forgave you.

EPHESIANS 4:31–32 NIV

• • •

Nine-year-old tomcat Chester was like a grumpy old man. If you nudged him off his favorite spot on the sofa, he hissed at you. If you scolded him for eating the dog's food, he whined and complained. Once, he even clawed a guest who simply sat in the wrong place.

After a while, Jana couldn't justify having him around her younger children. Chester proved to be too volatile. You never knew when he might start hissing or baring his teeth. She kept him in a separate room from the family, just to be safe. She didn't like to live this way, but what could she do?

Jana blamed Chester's anger issues on old age, but (truth be told) a lot of it came from getting his own way for so long. If you dared to cross him, he pitched a fit.

Maybe you know a few people like that. Or maybe you've been like that! Perhaps you've pitched a fit that you later regretted. Afterward, you thought, "Why did I let it get to me? Why did I get mad over the dinner plans or which movie to choose? It was supposed to be a fun evening out with friends, not a battle that I had to win at any cost."

We've all been there.

God never intended for His kids to get away with volatile tempers. In fact, He calls us to coolness of head and heart. Today, if you're dealing with issues of anger or bitterness, let them go. The Lord will take that anger and wash it away, in Jesus' name.

Lord, I'm ready to let go of the
anger I've held on to. And God, please
help me not to become an angry cat.
Show me how to defuse situations as they
arise in my heart so that I never hurt
others with my words or actions.

AMEN.

IF CATS COULD TALK, THEY WOULDN'T.

Nan Porter

Eye on the Prize

*You keep him in perfect peace whose mind is
stayed on you, because he trusts in you.*

ISAIAH 26:3 ESV

• • •

After Kathleen's husband left for work each morning, she
rolled back over in bed for an additional hour of sleep.
With her alarm set for seven thirty, she would catch a few
extra z's before having to start her day. Her cat, Weston,
didn't seem particularly happy with this arrangement. He
was raring to go, not drift back off to sleep.

At first Kathleen didn't really pick up on the ornery
cat's cues about his unhappiness with her morning routine, but after he started clawing at her comforter, she
realized his impatience might be an issue. So, to buy herself more time, she offered him a toy before going back
to sleep. Still, Weston refused to cooperate. He decided
to get even by sitting on the pillow next to Kathleen, just
staring, staring, staring intently at her as she slept. She
would awake with a startle, the cat's beady eyes intently
hyper-focused on her own. Talk about disconcerting!
Kathleen tried putting her own pillow over her head to
drown out the sound of the pitiful meows, but she finally
gave up.

Weston got one thing right: he kept his eye on the prize. He wouldn't move until Kathleen moved. He wouldn't start his day without her leading.

We could take a few cues from Weston, couldn't we? How many times do we take off on our own, not waiting for the Master to lead the way? We get impatient. We stare at heaven and wonder, "Will God ever wake up? Is He going to answer my prayer request or what?"

God always moves. He just does it in His time. And He never sleeps. The Bible says He's always awake and aware of what we're going through. So trust His timing and keep your eyes focused on Him, no matter how long you have to wait.

Lord, I won't give up. I won't step out ahead of You! I'll focus on You, Father, no matter how long it takes.

AMEN.

The Cat That Got the Cream

*Or do you not know that your body is a temple
of the Holy Spirit within you, whom you have
from God? You are not your own.*

I CORINTHIANS 6:19 ESV

• • •

Lucy affectionately named her tiger-striped cat Tigger. As a kitten, Tigger exhibited boundless energy. He would chase his own shadow and leap from one piece of furniture to another, and he especially enjoyed being teased with the fake mouse toy that Lucy purchased. All in all, his activity level kept the whole house hopping.

As he aged, Tigger slowed down. He started craving more and more food—even getting demanding about it at times. He would slam his empty bowl against the wall until Lucy filled it. He also enjoyed bowls of cream. Skim milk wouldn't do. Oh, no. He wanted the real deal. To make matters worse, Tigger's activity slowed almost to a halt. By the time he reached six years of age, the vet expressed some concerns. Tigger was no longer a tiger. These days, he looked and acted more like a couch potato with a paunchy midsection. As much as she hated to do it, Lucy put her precious kitty on a diet and exercise plan.

Maybe you can relate to Tigger. As a younger person, you were fit. Active. You watched what you ate and led a healthy lifestyle. These days, though . . . not so much. You'd rather ask "What's for dinner? Pizza, anyone?" than contemplate a lean piece of meat or salad.

There are lessons to be learned from that lazy kitty! It's never too late to turn things around. Today would be a terrific day to start. Up and at 'em, sister! Purge that fridge and take a walk around the block. God will surely put the tiger back in your tank if you do.

God, I don't want to squander my health or waste any of the days you've given me. If there are areas of my life that need tweaking, then tweak away, Father! It won't be easy, but I submit this body (and my desires) to You.

AMEN.

19

Pounce!

With all humility and gentleness, with patience,
bearing with one another in love, eager to maintain
the unity of the Spirit in the bond of peace.

EPHESIANS 4:2–3 ESV

• • •

You could only describe the cat that lived next door to Brenda one way: evil. The gorgeous black and white feline was deceptively beautiful. But this handsome little fellow had a more sinister side, and Brenda had experienced it firsthand. Now, when she looked at him, Brenda just wanted to run in the opposite direction.

Unfortunately, little Precious—who was inappropriately named—saw Brenda as something of a target. Many times, he would jump from the roof overhead, scaring her to death as he landed right in front of her. Once he popped out from behind the plant stand on her front porch and attacked her leg, claws fully extended. Still another time he shot out from under her car as she opened the driver's-side door. Brenda quickly jumped into the driver's seat to avoid getting attacked.

These pouncing episodes became so problematic that Brenda finally had no choice. She had to talk to the neighbor about it. Unfortunately, that neighbor saw Precious as nothing but, well, precious. She didn't take the complaint seriously.

Maybe you know what it's like to be pounced upon. You're going along through life and all is well, and then, from out of the blue . . . pounce! Calamity hits. It brings with it hissing and screaming and gnashing of teeth. Well, maybe not all those things, but it brings chaos and confusion and often an abundance of pain. You're startled, confused, and hurt. And you're also scared to keep moving ahead because you think it might happen again.

Pounces happen. They're a part of life. But God doesn't want you to live in fear, anticipating the next attack. Settle into Him. Trust that He'll be there when the bad moments come. He will, you know. And He will work all things for good, even the not-so-precious things.

Lord, I don't want to live in fear,
waiting for the next shoe to drop.
Today I choose to trust You, my
Protector and my Friend.

AMEN.

Pet Peeve

Do nothing out of selfish ambition or vain conceit.
Rather, in humility value others above yourselves.

PHILIPPIANS 2:3 NIV

• • •

Elizabeth's cat Maggie had an inordinate fear of automobiles. The usually mild-mannered cat would lose it every time she was placed in a vehicle of any kind. Elizabeth couldn't be sure whether the motion of the car or the view of the other vehicles whipping by outside caused the trauma. The poor cat seemed to be triggered whenever Elizabeth turned the key in the ignition.

Elizabeth began to crate Maggie every time she put her in the car and to cover the crate with a dark cloth. Elizabeth still heard some fussing from the frightened kitty, but soon Maggie's reactions were not nearly as bad as before.

Maybe you know what it's like to feel traumatized. Something bad happened to you and now, whenever you're placed in precarious positions, you're immediately transported back in time to the awful event. Unfortunately, these little triggers are really hampering your walk with God and with others.

The Lord wants to release you from the pain of the past and free you up for the journey ahead. He doesn't want you to simply avoid those triggers; rather, He wants you to be completely and totally healed so that when you face them, the same fears don't erupt.

What triggers you most these days? Take a closer look at those things. Write them down. Think about why you're so volatile when those things happen. Then give that list to the Lord. Ask Him to cover each and every thing (much like Elizabeth covered Maggie's crate). He'll do it if you ask. He can calm your spirit so that your reactions (both external and internal) are subdued.

Lord, I give these triggers to You. There are things that really hurt (and/or bug) me, but I won't use them as excuses to panic. Thank You for freeing me up so that I can take the journey in peace, Father.

AMEN.

21

Outsmarted by the Cat

Can a man hide himself in secret places so
that I cannot see him? declares the LORD.
Do I not fill heaven and earth? declares the LORD.

JEREMIAH 23:24 ESV

• • •

Kimba was a sneaky little thing. Whenever her owner, Emily, left for the day, Kimba had free rein of the house, and she took full advantage of it. She discovered a purse hanging from a hook in the bedroom. That looked interesting. She found a sock one of the kids had left on the floor. That looked fun too.

Day after day, Kimba began to store up goodies for herself. She hid them in the closet behind that big noisy machine her owner used to clean the floors. Kimba stashed away a watch, a couple of pencils from the desk, a scrub pad, and even a charm bracelet she'd found on the dresser. What fun! The thrills kept up as she snagged even more goodies after that.

It didn't take long for Emily to figure out why all her things were disappearing. While cleaning out the closet one day, she happened upon Kimba's secret stash.

"You little rascal!" She scolded the kitty and then gathered her belongings. "Guess I'll have to do a better job of putting things away."

Kimba's sneaky behavior is a bit like ours when we're hiding out from God. We sneak into our own little bubble, thinking we're out of His view. Once there, we allow ourselves to commit sinful acts we'd never think of doing in public.

Unlike Kimba's situation with Emily, we're never out of God's sight. He sees all that's done in secret. And it doesn't take long for the "You little rascal!" feelings to come, once you realize He's on to you.

Fortunately, God is gracious and forgiving, ready to give you a cuddle and a fresh start. So, live in the light, sister! No more hiding away in the shadows for you!

Lord, I'll stick to the light.
I won't sneak back into those
old patterns. Help me, I pray.

AMEN.

22

Curiosity Killed the Cat

Submit yourselves therefore to God.
Resist the devil, and he will flee from you.

JAMES 4:7 ESV

• • •

Buster—a short-haired tabby cat—loved his life on the farm. He was right at home with the goats, the cows, and the chickens. They didn't bother him a bit, though he did his best to irritate them from time to time.

Buster loved to hang out in the barn near the horse stalls. He had to watch his step, since the big monsters had almost trampled him a time or two. Still, he learned how and when to approach.

Only one problem with the horse stalls—the flies. Buster didn't mind them too much, but his master, Katie, did. She had hung sticky fly tape above each stall in an attempt to snag the pesky little critters.

One day, one of the fly tapes floated to the ground below without anyone's knowledge. Buster accidentally stepped on it, and before he knew what hit him, he found himself stuck. No matter what he did, he couldn't shake that sticky trap from his right front paw. Thank goodness Katie rushed to his rescue. She set him free, once and for all.

Maybe you've felt stuck a time or two as well. You didn't mean to get yourself into that predicament, but before you knew it, there was no way out and no one to help you. Then, in a miraculous answer to prayer, your Master swept in and saved the day, pulling you from that trap and setting things aright. What a wonderful heavenly Father, to care so much for His children!

Lord, I'm so grateful for the many times You've pulled me out of sticky situations. When I couldn't save myself, You were right there, ready to release me from the very things that held me bound. How wonderful You are, heavenly Father!

AMEN.

23

Paw-sibility

Jesus looked at them and said, "With man this is impossible, but with God all things are possible."

MATTHEW 19:26 NIV

• • •

Peyton took one look at the two-week-old litter of kittens and her heart broke. With their mother now deceased, how would the little ones survive? As a volunteer at the shelter, she often opted to take on difficult cases, fostering until they were well enough to be adopted. But this? This looked impossible to her. These three babies were fragile and sickly and would need round-the-clock care.

With a bold determination, she decided to take on the task of caring for them. Unfortunately, one of the babies was just too weak and passed away a couple of days later. But the other two, tiny and weak as they were, did pretty well with the bottle feedings. After a week or so, Peyton saw progress and dared herself to hope. Then the week after that, they were alert and moving around their little bed like normal kittens.

She kept them until they were eight weeks old. The families who adopted them would never know all she had endured to save their little lives. But she would never forget the experience or the joy of watching their transformation.

Peyton took on a seemingly impossible task, didn't she? Perhaps you're facing something that feels just as huge. In the natural, it seems unlikely you'll succeed. Oh, but when you add God to the equation, the impossible becomes possible!

Don't give up, even if the mountain you're facing looms large in front of you. Don't quit. Ask God to join you in the battle and trust that He's on your side. Before long, what is fragile and weak will be healthy and strong, if you don't give up.

Lord, I won't quit! I'll keep going, even when things look bleak. May I never forget that with You nothing is impossible.

AMEN.

24

Fat Cat

Do not lay up for yourselves treasures on earth, where moth and rust destroy and where thieves break in and steal, but lay up for yourselves treasures in heaven, where neither moth nor rust destroys and where thieves do not break in and steal. For where your treasure is, there your heart will be also.

MATTHEW 6:19–21 ESV

• • •

When Carol's neighbor Susan passed away, her cat—lovingly referred to as Fat Cat by everyone in the neighborhood—needed a home. But taking on the docile kitty might prove to be a big task for whoever decided to adopt him. He was, after all, more than twenty pounds overweight. Susan, who had battled cancer for more than two years, had spoiled the little feline—filling his heart and his tummy. But now the consequences stared Carol in the face. Could she tackle such a big challenge?

After talking it over with her husband, the family adopted Fat Cat. Carol started an immediate "trimming down" routine that included lots of play and activity time. She bought a little laser pen so that Fat Cat could chase the light. What fun he had, running after that tiny flicker of light.

Carol purchased other fun toys and kept him busy as much as possible. She also put his food in hard-to-reach areas, so that he would have to climb to get to it. And the amount of food was far less than what he had grown accustomed to. Fat Cat didn't seem to mind too much. He enjoyed the added activities and stimulation, especially chasing that little light. Over time, he dropped the weight and went on to live a long, healthy life.

Maybe you're like Fat Cat. You're easily distracted—by bright and shiny objects, by relationships, by finances, by aspirations. Perhaps you chase these things in the same way Fat Cat chased that silly little pen light. Here and there you run, only to realize you've lost sight of the goal.

Today God wants you to look to Him, the only true Light. He's never-changing, ever-faithful, and ready to guide you wherever you need to go.

Lord, I'll keep my eyes wide open so that I'm not distracted by the wrong things. I want to follow hard after You, not after those "flickering lights" that threaten to turn my head. I will follow You, my Light and my Lord.

AMEN.

DOGS HAVE OWNERS.
CATS HAVE STAFF.

Anonymous

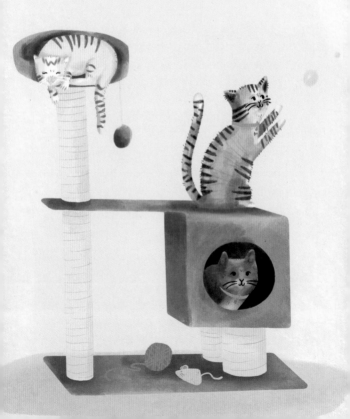

25

A Purr-fectly Wonderful Perspective

Not that I am speaking of being in need, for I have learned in whatever situation I am to be content. I know how to be brought low, and I know how to abound. In any and every circumstance, I have learned the secret of facing plenty and hunger, abundance and need.

PHILIPPIANS 4:11–12 ESV

• • •

When you think of the word *contentment*, what comes to mind? Do you picture yourself seated in front of a roaring fireplace on a winter's day with a blanket over your lap and a good book in your hand? Do your circumstances have to be extraordinary in order for you to feel truly content, or can you conjure up those feelings when the kids are crying, bills need paying, and the homeowner's association is mad because you need to cut the grass?

Dahlia learned the true meaning of contentment from her cat, Gus. He was getting up there in years and had a host of medical problems. Still, the sweet old kitty didn't let that get to him. He had one place where all his problems faded away—curled up on Dahlia's lap. So, she granted him all the attention and love he craved. To see the look of contentment in his eyes, to hear that gentle purring as she stroked his head, served as a reminder that, even in the everydayness, even when things around you aren't perfect, it's still possible to be totally and fully content when you spend time with your Master.

No matter what's swirling around you—even if you're in a particularly difficult season right now—God longs for you to sense true contentment. It can only come when you lay those burdens down and draw close to Him. In that quiet, special place, ask God to let peace flood your soul. Ask Him to let you glimpse His perspective. In Him, you will find all the contentment you need to get through the day.

Lord, take away my discontentment! May I not become consumed with all that's not going right. Thank You for the reminder that I'm already blessed simply because I'm Your child.

AMEN.

26

A Telling Tail

Therefore, confess your sins to one another and pray for one another, that you may be healed. The prayer of a righteous person has great power as it is working.

JAMES 5:16 ESV

• • •

There's much to learn from a cat's tail. For instance, if your kitty's tail is held high up in the air, she's perfectly at home in her environment, completely content and overly confident. She's also feeling friendly. Sometimes her tail curves, though, and you wonder what that means. If her tail is looking more like a question mark, she might be asking for your attention.

Be careful if that tail is pointed straight down! This might be a sign that your sweet baby is feeling angry or aggressive. An even bigger sign that she's angry might be a tail that's slapping back and forth rapidly. And if that tail is tucked between her legs, she's probably feeling scared or nervous. Another sign of fear is a puffed-up tail. This is an indicator that she's terrified or agitated.

Do you ever put off body signals like your feline does? Maybe you can't hide your displeasure when a friend at work gets a promotion but you don't. Or maybe you wish you could hide your jealousy when your sister and her husband buy that new mega-house and you're still living in the tiny starter home you bought twenty years ago.

We show all kinds of emotions in our expressions. Anger at a spouse or child. Worry when the bills aren't paid. Frustration when things aren't going our way. Sometimes people read our body language and think, "Hey, where's her faith? I thought she was supposed to be a believer." Maybe it's time to reexamine the message we're sending and ask God to fill us to overflowing with His Spirit, so that He is the only expression others see.

Lord, I don't want to come across as a grump. Or an angry person. Or someone who is constantly frustrated. I want to be a vessel for Your Spirit, filled to overflowing, so that You can shine through me for all to see.

AMEN.

27

Like Something the Cat Dragged In

As each has received a gift, use it to serve one another, as good stewards of God's varied grace: whoever speaks, as one who speaks oracles of God; whoever serves, as one who serves by the strength that God supplies—in order that in everything God may be glorified through Jesus Christ. To him belong glory and dominion forever and ever. Amen.

I PETER 4:10–11 ESV

• • •

Ingrid lived alone and was happy for the company of her cat, Fiesta. The little feline remained active, even as she aged. One morning, Ingrid walked out onto the back porch and gasped when she saw a dead mouse on the mat. What in the world? She disposed of it and tried to put it out of her mind.

A few weeks later, she found a dead bird on the mat in the same spot. Things were starting to make sense now. Fiesta had taken to killing these little ones and bringing them as offerings to her owner.

The pattern continued for several months. Every so often, Ingrid found the carcass of a bird or mouse on the mat. Instead of scolding the kitty, Ingrid came to accept the gifts for what they were—an offering.

Sometimes our offerings to God are a bit like that. We bring Him the smelly dead areas of our lives, the things we wouldn't want others to see. Instead of scolding us for creating the messes, He disposes of the trash and encourages us to keep digging deeper, to come up with even more things in our lives that need to be discarded.

What offerings can you give the Lord today? Are there smelly areas that need purging? Are there secrets you haven't wanted to acknowledge? Bring them to the mat. Drop them. Ask for His help, His power, His grace. He will surely accept your meager offerings as a token of great love and affection and will offer nothing but affection in return.

Lord, sometimes I feel like I don't have much to offer. I'm such a mess. But You love me in my mess, Father, and that brings my heart such joy. How I love and worship You!

AMEN.

28

Catnip

No temptation has overtaken you except what is common to mankind. And God is faithful; He will not let you be tempted beyond what you can bear. But when you are tempted, He will also provide a way out so that you can endure it.

• • •

Paula learned early on that a little catnip goes a long way. She bought some for her kitten as a diversion, to keep the little one occupied. But Muffin fell in love with the stuff. Before long, she demanded it with loud wails and cries. Paula had a hard time figuring out how much was too much. After all, the stuff proved to be somewhat potent and sometimes caused an upset tummy for her kitty. Still, it broke her heart to hear her baby cry, so she often gave in.

Maybe you've battled a temptation like Muffin. You've had a little of something you enjoyed—alcohol, drugs, sugary sweets—and wanted more. Your "occasional" became every day. And before long, you were so hooked it was hard to give those things up.

Too much catnip makes the kitty sick, and too much of any vice can wreak havoc in a human's life as well—

not just physically but emotionally and spiritually. Some people become so addicted to their catnip that they put their relationships and even their families at risk.

What is God asking you to lay down today? What's your catnip? Maybe you read that sentence and think, "Well, that's silly. I'm not addicted to anything that's dangerous." Don't be so sure. Do you spend too much time with a negative friend, perhaps? Have you taken on some of her habits? Do you overspend, buying things that are unnecessary? Do you go back for that second slice of cake? Are you prone to gossip?

Catnip comes in all sorts of packages. And remember, what might seem harmless at first can rapidly develop into a habit that's hard to break.

Lord, I'll give up my catnip!
There are all sorts of little guilty
pleasures I've enjoyed that aren't good
for me. Reveal them and show me how
to purge them from my life, I pray.

AMEN.

29

Catnaps

Come to me, all who labor and are heavy laden, and I will give you rest. Take my yoke upon you, and learn from me, for I am gentle and lowly in heart, and you will find rest for your souls. For my yoke is easy, and my burden is light.

MATTHEW 11:28–30 ESV

• • •

Callie envied her cat. The little thing had nothing more to do with her life than to lounge around and sun herself, day after day. Oh, Genevieve would occasionally rouse herself from her slumber to nibble on some kibble, but then she would go right back to her spot on the back of the sofa, where beams of sunlight streamed through the window and lulled her into yet another sleep.

"Wish I could take a little snooze," Callie would say as she happened by with a basket of laundry on her way to the washing machine.

"Must be nice," she would add as she buzzed by with an armload of kids' toys, headed to the toy box.

Maybe you can relate to Callie's woes. There's never a moment to catch your breath because your workload is too high. You wish life would offer you the opportunity to lounge around, but it doesn't seem possible.

Today, God is asking you to reconsider your schedule. He's got big things for you to do, sure. But you're going to need the energy to accomplish all that He has set before you. Supernatural energy only comes from one source—time in His presence.

If you'll set your gaze on your heavenly Father, He will draw you into that holy place with Him. There you will be encouraged to hand over the things that have worn you down. He will show you how to bring all areas of your life into balance, so that rest—true rest—is possible.

Lord, I feel like I'm always on the go. I buzz from here to there, getting a lot done. But I secretly envy those who move at a slower pace. I wonder how they manage. Show me how to bring things in balance. I long to spend time with You and to receive the kind of peace and rest that only You can offer. Help me, I pray.

AMEN.

30

Easy, Tiger

As a prisoner for the Lord, then, I urge you to
live a life worthy of the calling you have received.
Be completely humble and gentle; be patient,
bearing with one another in love. Make every effort
to keep the unity of the Spirit through the bond of peace.

EPHESIANS 4:1–3 NIV

• • •

Lisa paced the living room after hanging up the phone. Her thoughts were in a whirl. "Oooh, that Brenda is so stubborn and pushy! It's got to be her way or the highway. I can never give any ideas or suggestions. It's pointless to try to work with her."

Maybe you've known a few Brendas in your day. You've tried to work with them, but they just plowed right over you, taking the lead (whether qualified for the task or not). What is it that makes some people such steamrollers? Ugh!

In many ways pushy people are reminiscent of two cats trying to live together in a house, each set on having his own way. Cats will insist on their own turf—their toys, their bed, their spot on the sofa. Those naughty kitties will hiss, fight, and butt heads if anyone dares tread in their space. They would rather fight than give an inch. This stubborn behavior can make everyone around them uncomfortable.

Easy, tiger! Don't be a headbutter. It definitely changes the mood in the room when you push people around. Make sure you're known by all as a woman seasoned by grace, ready and willing to let others take the lead, especially if you're not called to be in charge. And if you're dealing with a headbutter, pray. It might be time to back away from her altogether or to ask your boss to put you on a different team at work. The goal, as always, is balance in all things, even relationships like these.

Lord, I've dealt with some bossy people in my day. They've made my life very uncomfortable. And—just to keep it real—I've been a little bossy, too. Please forgive me and show me a better way, Father.

AMEN.

31

Clawful

Do you not know that in a race all the runners run, but only one gets the prize? Run in such a way as to get the prize.

I CORINTHIANS 9:24 NIV

• • •

Tricia stopped at the master bedroom door and gasped as she surveyed the scene in front of her. It looked a bit like Christmas morning, with snow covering the ground. Only, this happened to be toilet paper—lots and lots of toilet paper.

She waded through it to the bathroom, where she found the empty roll still in place next to the toilet.

"Conner!" She called out the cat's name, but he didn't show up. That little monster. She searched high and low, finally finding him under the bed. "You come out of there. We need to talk about this." The cat refused to budge.

You can scold a cat all day long for making a mess like that, but one thing you can't do is expect even the most repentant of kitties to clean up his mess. He wouldn't even know where to begin.

What about you? Have you made messes and then expected others to clean up after you? What toilet paper have you shredded lately?

When you make a mess of things—and let's admit it, we all do—you need to stick around for the cleanup. Do the right thing. Make apologies, sure, but then go the distance to make things right after the fact. God loves it when we go the extra mile to make things right. Doing so will also help maintain relationships with those you love.

Are there any messes you still need to clean up? Don't let another day go by. Pray, and God will get you through it. Before long, everything will be tidy again.

Lord, I've made a few messes in my day.
Without You, cleanup would be impossible.
But I want to do the right thing, Father.
Don't let me slink off into the shadows when
I mess up. Help me, I pray.

AMEN.

32

Furr Real

*Do not conform to the pattern of this world,
but be transformed by the renewing of your mind.
Then you will be able to test and approve what God's
will is—His good, pleasing and perfect will.*

ROMANS 12:2 NIV

• • •

Jenny stared at the various cats in their shelter cages. They all looked pretty much alike, though a few were different in color. Picking out the perfect one might be tricky. Should she base her decision on looks or personality?

She continued to peruse the aisle of the shelter until she came upon a cage with the strangest-looking cat inside.

"Excuse me!" she called out to the volunteer who was feeding the animals. "This is a . . . cat?"

"Yes." The woman smiled. "That's Cleopatra. She's a Sphynx. They're actually very expensive. Her owner passed away, and the family brought Cleo in just this morning."

"Oh, wow." Jenny gave the unusual-looking animal a closer look. "Her ears are very . . . pronounced."

"Yes, and her coloring is really pretty. And check out those lemon-shaped eyes. Aren't they gorgeous?"

Jenny had to admit they were pretty. In fact, after a few moments of staring at Cleopatra, she decided she couldn't live without her.

Maybe you feel like Cleo at times. You look different from the other women. There are certain body parts that feel more pronounced than they should be. You feel as if you stick out like a sore thumb.

Remember, God didn't make His girls to be cookie-cutter images of one another. Cleopatra had great worth . . . and so do you, sister. Don't let the mirror define that worth. Let the One who gazes lovingly into your eyes tell you just how much value you have.

I won't let the mirror define me, Lord! You have created me in Your image and You think I'm beautiful. I'll do my best to base my value on Your thoughts, not my own.

AMEN.

AS EVERY CAT
OWNER KNOWS,
NOBODY OWNS A CAT.

Ellen Perry Berkeley

33

Stick the Landing

So now finish doing it as well, so that your
readiness in desiring it may be matched by
your completing it out of what you have.

II CORINTHIANS 8:11 ESV

. . .

Meg got tired just watching her Himalayan cat, Luna. The feisty feline couldn't seem to stay in one place for long. She jumped up onto her scratch tower, then got bored and leaped down onto the sofa, sticking the landing and convincing Meg she was going to stay put. After just a few minutes, however, Luna would yawn, stretch, and hop down onto the floor, where she would pace the room. Back to the sofa she would go. Then down to the floor.

After continuing on like this for a while, Luna rubbed up against Meg's ankles.

"What's wrong, girl?" Meg asked. "Why are you so restless? What's up with that?"

The cat continued to wind herself around her owner's feet. She just couldn't seem to stay put.

Maybe you know what that feels like. You can't seem to stay put once you've started something, no matter how hard you try. You dive into a diet but give up a few days in. You join a book club but drop out after only a couple of weeks. You tell yourself you're going to get up early to get a few things done but hit the snooze button instead. You agree to meet your neighbor for a long walk through the neighborhood to get your steps in but back out at the last minute because you're tired. You're determined to read more of your Bible but convince yourself you can't.

God wants us to be consistent, not just in our walk with Him but in every area of our lives. Our diet, work, sleep, family time . . . all of it needs to be under His submission. What projects have you started but not completed? When you give those areas of your life to God, you're much more likely to finish well.

Lord, I don't want to be restless.
Give me the focus I need to finish the
things I've started. Help me, I pray.

AMEN.

34

Nine Lives

The Lord is not slow in keeping His promise,
as some understand slowness. Instead He is
patient with you, not wanting anyone to perish,
but everyone to come to repentance.

II PETER 3:9 NIV

...

Connie lived in a third-floor apartment with her cat, Lucky. She often left the window cracked so that Lucky could get some fresh air while she was at work. He particularly loved to sit in the window and watch the traffic on the busy city street below. Never once did Connie consider the open window a hazard. It had a tight screen in place, after all, and the cat never messed with that.

One day Connie received a call at work that shook her to the core. Lucky had somehow made it through the mesh screen and had fallen three stories to the ground below. Her neighbor found the cat crying on the sidewalk and rushed him in to the nearest vet.

Connie could not shake the feelings of guilt as she rushed to the vet's office. She found her sweet baby in good hands and almost couldn't believe her ears when she learned his injuries were mostly superficial. Lucky lived up to his name that day! He got a second chance. Talk about a cat with nine lives! Lucky used up one that day, for sure.

Maybe you know what it feels like to get an unexpected second chance. It had nothing to do with luck, did it? That opportunity was a divine gift, straight from your heavenly Father, who loves His kids enough to offer chance after chance, even when we get it wrong.

Today, think back over all the second chances God has given you, then begin to praise Him for every opportunity to begin again. And if you're in a position where you need a second chance right now, just ask. He's waiting to spring into action on your behalf.

Lord, I've had too many second chances to count! You've been so good to me. When I didn't deserve it, You brought me back from the abyss. What a gracious God You are!

AMEN.

35

Cat's in the Cradle

Finally, be strong in the Lord and in His mighty power. Put on the full armor of God, so that you can take your stand against the devil's schemes.

EPHESIANS 6:10–11 NIV

• • •

Cats are delightful little beings, but they can also be a hazard in some situations. Jenna found this out the hard way when her baby daughter was born. No sooner did she bring little Addy home from the hospital than her cat, Chloe, tried to get a little too close. Jenna did her best to shoo her away, but the cat persisted. She wanted to be right up in the baby's face, offering her full adoration and attention.

Jenna had already done her research. She knew that cats and newborns don't mix. The risk of suffocation is too high. So, for several months she had to completely separate her sweet kitty from that precious baby girl. Boundaries were put in place and strictly enforced.

God wants us to put similar boundaries in our lives. We don't always realize when the enemy is in our midst, but he's there, hoping to wreak havoc in our lives. Sometimes we invite him in without even realizing what we're doing.

Today, take inventory. Are there any lines in the sand you need to address? Perhaps you've allowed others to cross boundaries into your personal space and you've paid a price for their intrusion. Or maybe you've allowed negative thoughts too much headspace. Regardless, it's never too late to put boundaries in place.

Take inventory, then ask God to help you place the necessary boundaries, not just for your safety and sanity, but to bless those around you as well.

Lord, I need boundaries in certain areas of my life! Please shine Your spotlight on the many areas where I need to be more cautious, and then give me the tenacity and courage to make the necessary changes.

AMEN.

36

All Bark and No Bite

But He said to me, "My grace is sufficient for you, for My power is made perfect in weakness." Therefore I will boast all the more gladly about my weaknesses, so that Christ's power may rest on me. That is why, for Christ's sake, I delight in weaknesses, in insults, in hardships, in persecutions, in difficulties. For when I am weak, then I am strong.

II CORINTHIANS 12:9-10 NIV

• • •

Fluffy stared out the living room window every day at her backyard. Her owner, Casey, let her out there on occasion but only when she could keep a close eye on her. Still, Fluffy dreamed of climbing over the fence and exploring whatever glorious things might be on the other side.

One day she found her opportunity. Casey's youngest son left the back door cracked open and Fluffy slid right through. She slunk across the yard, headed straight for the fence. It took more strength than she had imagined to get to the top of it, but once she did, victory! She could see right into the neighbor's yard. Talk about lovely! Those gardens! That pool! Wow! Fluffy could hardly wait to begin her adventure into the unknown.

She had just started to leap down into the grass when

ferocious barking began. Two huge dogs—a rottweiler and a German shepherd—confronted her. Oh, help! Fluffy froze in place, her little heart pounding, and finally did the only thing that made sense: she jumped down into her own yard and headed straight for the door.

Maybe you know what it feels like to face the big dogs. You've braved the great unknown, climbed the fence, and you're about ready to take that leap of faith. But then fear sets in, and all of a sudden you feel terrified and frozen in your tracks. "What happened?" you ask yourself. "How did I get here?"

We can't let the lies of insecurities block us from what God has for us. They are all bark and no bite. So, don't let them frighten you from the things God has called you to. Have courage, sister! There are places to go and people to see, after all.

Lord, I'll move in faith and won't let fear stop me at the fence. I'll tune out the bark of the enemy and focus on You instead. Help me overcome any adversities as I step out in faith toward what You've called me to.

AMEN.

37

Cat-astrophe

There is therefore now no condemnation for those who are in Christ Jesus.

ROMANS 8:1 ESV

• • •

It took Isabel hours to paint her kitchen cabinets. She had to sand them down, prime them, and then put on two coats of paint. What a job! The task took a full day, but she was so happy with the outcome. How lovely her kitchen looked, so fresh and new. She could hardly wait to show it off to her friends and loved ones.

When Isabel turned her back to wash the brushes, her tabby cat, Felix, rubbed up against the wet paint. Isabel didn't even notice the hairs stuck on the front of the cabinet door until later. A streak of white paint covered the kitty's right side. What a cat-astrophe!

Felix wasn't happy about the bath that followed, and Isabel didn't enjoy touching up the paint job, but both tasks eventually got done. Felix walked away wiser (and wetter), and Isabel walked away with the knowledge that she would keep a closer eye on her kitty next time. Lessons learned on both ends!

Maybe you've walked a mile in Felix's shoes. You've

accidentally gotten yourself into a mess and it has left its mark. You didn't mean for it to happen. You didn't want it to happen. And you certainly wish you could remove all traces of it. But there it is—a reminder of the mistake you made or the accident you wish you'd avoided.

Not everything goes according to plan. We make mistakes. And sometimes life hands us things that are beyond our control. Instead of hyper-focusing on the accident (or mistake), allow God to dip you into the sink and wash away that stain, once and for all.

Lord, when it comes to mistakes, I've made some whoppers. How good and kind You've been to pick me up, wash me off, and give me a clean start. Have I mentioned how grateful I am? Thank You, Father!

AMEN.

38

Cat and Mouse

I appeal to you, brothers, to watch out for those who cause
divisions and create obstacles contrary to the doctrine that
you have been taught; avoid them. For such persons do not
serve our Lord Christ, but their own appetites, and by smooth
talk and flattery they deceive the hearts of the naive.

ROMANS 16:17–18 ESV

. . .

Frick and Frack were brothers from the same litter of Siamese kittens. As babies, Frick always picked on Frack. Things didn't improve as they got older. Both were adopted together, and Frick continued his dominance over his brother at every turn. For the most part, they got along well together—they played, slept, and lounged around peacefully. But whenever push came to shove, Frick did the pushing and shoving and Frack simply let him. Their little games of cat and mouse were fun, as long as Frack was always the mouse.

Maybe you can relate. There's a Frick in your life, always demanding, exerting, insisting. Or maybe you're the one always exerting dominance on others. These things happen, especially inside families. But, why?

It's not always easy to live together in the same house (or small social circle) with others, is it? And why is it that we're usually hardest on the ones we're closest to? We're not as likely to guard our words or our actions in our own home, certainly not as cautious as we would be, say, at church.

Have you ever hurt those you love? Do you tend to be harder on one person than the others? Perhaps God is calling you aside today to ask you not to dominate others. Stop the cat-and-mouse games. Don't demean or demand. Instead, ask the Lord for better ways to communicate with the ones you're struggling with. It is possible to live in unity, even with those who get on your nerves.

Lord, it hurts to be demeaned.
I've been there. But I've also been the
one with the sharp tongue at times,
especially with my loved ones. Help me better
communicate Your heart, Father. Today I
lay down my desire to always be right
and trust that You have a better way.

AMEN.

39

Top Dog

*Talk no more so very proudly, let not arrogance
come from your mouth; for the LORD is a God of
knowledge, and by him actions are weighed.*

I SAMUEL 2:3 ESV

• • •

God determined which animals would dominate others.
Put a lion and a Chihuahua in the same room, and one
will certainly have more sway than the other. (Though, to
be fair, Chihuahuas are a handful and can stand on their
own four paws.)

Where do cats fall in the grand scheme of things?
If you put a cat in a room with a tiger, a bear, or even
a pit bull, what would happen? If you were to ask a cat
owner, they would say that most cats think they're the
top dog, pun intended. They have a superiority complex
that gives them an uncanny fearlessness. They're bold
beyond reason and most (if they could speak) would tell
you that they rule the roost. Disagree with them and they
would simply look down their noses at you.

Know any people like that? Some folks always seem
to have more power than the rest, don't they? Many
have an air of superiority about them, as if to say, "I'm
the top dog here."

God is not a fan of arrogance. He wants you to be an equal opportunity lover of people, no matter where they fall in the lineup. From the lowest of the low to the highest of the high, God has called you to treat everyone the same. That means you can't favor the woman in leadership any more than the one paid to scrub the toilets.

The only One worthy of true headship in your life is the King of kings and Lord of lords, the Lion of Judah. Put Him in His rightful place and He'll show you exactly who's top dog.

Lord, people with a superiority complex bug me. They come across as arrogant. They're hard to be around. Show me how to help them, I pray. And while we're at it, Lord, if there's any arrogance in me, please rid me of it today.

AMEN.

40

The Things We
Leave Behind

For we are to God the pleasing aroma of Christ among
those who are being saved and those who are perishing.

II CORINTHIANS 2:15 NIV

• • •

With that silky long white coat, Phoebe looked picture-
perfect, like something out of a cat lover's magazine.
And her docile, gentle nature made her even more adorable. Her owner, Linda, felt she'd won the jackpot with
this one.

Only one problem—Phoebe shed. A lot. After letting
the sweet kitty spend time in her lap, Linda's black slacks
were covered with white hair.

Everywhere you looked in the house, you saw more
of the hair—on the sofa, on the comforter, even on the
floor. Little piles of white fluff greeted you, no matter
where you went. And, as much as she swept, Linda had
to wonder if she'd ever manage to keep up with it all.
Though she didn't mean to, Phoebe left something
behind everywhere she went, and it caused grief for her
owner.

Here's a question for you to consider today: What are you leaving behind? When you walk out of a room filled with people, what fragrance have you left in the air? Do people say, "Thank goodness she's gone, I couldn't take much more of her mouth!" or are they saying, "There's something so amazing about her. She always makes me feel so positive and hopeful"?

You might not realize you're leaving anything behind at all, but those who know and love you (and even those who simply tolerate you) might be quick to say, "She leaves something behind, all right."

Today, get real with God. Ask Him to shine His spotlight on areas of your life that might need tweaking. Do you gossip? Complain? Grumble about the boss day in and day out? Maybe it's time to stop shedding all that icky stuff and shed a little peace, love, and joy instead.

I want to leave behind a lovely aroma when I leave a room, Lord. I'll need Your help to do so, but I bend to Your will today.

AMEN.

YOU HAD ME
AT MEOW.

Anonymous

41

A Timely Treat

Therefore, my beloved brothers, be steadfast,
immovable, always abounding in the work of the Lord,
knowing that in the Lord your labor is not in vain.

I CORINTHIANS 15:58 ESV

• • •

Sylvia was blessed to work from home. She kept herself on a pretty regular schedule so that she would get the work done. Every morning she woke at about the same time, got prepared for her day, and settled into her chair to dive into her work. She took the usual lunch break and got back to work around one. Then, sometime around three in the afternoon she would break for a snack and for a quick aerobic workout to stay awake.

Sylvia's cat, Jasper, seemed to have her routine memorized. He knew the minute his food would go into the bowl in the morning, and he counted on a treat at three. One afternoon Sylvia deviated from her routine. She got caught up in her work and couldn't break away. Jasper wound his way around her ankles, distracting and irritating her.

"Not right now, boy," she said as she nudged him away. "I'm busy."

He disappeared, but she didn't give him much thought. Only when she found him sitting quietly next to the treat jar at four thirty did she realize he'd been patiently waiting for her all that time.

God wants us to be as consistent in our walk with Him as Jasper proved to be with his treats. He longs for us to meet Him every day—both in prayer and in His Word. He wants us to hover close and be ready for the blessings (think treats!) that He pours out. Most of all, He desires our love and companionship, day in and day out.

Lord, I'm doing my best to be consistent in my walk with You. Please show me areas that need tweaking. I'll be waiting, Lord, not for a blessing but for precious time with You.

AMEN.

42

Scaredy-Cat

*For the Spirit God gave us does not make us timid,
but gives us power, love and self-discipline.*

II TIMOTHY 1:7 NIV

. . .

Oscar hadn't lived with his new owner, Sandie, for long.
He was still getting to know the layout of the house and
all the people in it. Every day presented a flurry of activity as four kids dressed for school and their mom raced
around helping them.

Oscar's favorite time of day was midmorning when
Sandie would return from dropping the kids off at
school, grab a cup of coffee, and sit on the sofa to read
her Bible. He loved those cozy moments best because
he got to curl up next to her in total peace and quiet.

One morning, however, Sandie had different plans.
Instead of sitting on the sofa, she reached for this strange
machine—a large red thing with a handle. It seemed to
have something to do with the floor. She plugged it in
and seconds later the most awful sound filled the air!
Oscar's heart started racing as the horrible machine
shrieked out a noise that made his ears ache. He ran
from the room and hid under the bed until the painful
sound went away.

Maybe you feel Oscar's pain. You're easily spooked by things. Noises. Being alone in the house. You're even frightened of everyday things like bills and taxes. Sometimes your boss scares you. And, for sure, that one friend who's so erratic can cause a shiver of fear to go up your spine.

God gave you a spirit not of fear but rather of power, love, and a sound mind. That means you can work your way through the fear and trust Him to keep you safe. It also means you can maintain your sanity as the two of you power through together.

Lord, I'm timid at times. I get afraid.
Thank You for the reminder that You
haven't given me a spirit of fear.
With Your help I can be brave!

AMEN.

43

Tattletale Cat

My brothers, if anyone among you wanders from the truth and someone brings him back, let him know that whoever brings back a sinner from his wandering will save his soul from death and will cover a multitude of sins.

JAMES 5:19–20 ESV

. . .

Mary's kids couldn't get away with anything because the cat always told on them. If they got into a squabble in the bedroom, Frizzie—the tattletale feline—would come straight to Mary and wouldn't stop meowing until she got her attention. Mary would follow on the cat's tail into the bedroom to discover the quarreling kids.

Once, Frizzie even stomped his foot when Mary wasn't paying attention to his usual meows. He had something important to tell her—a delivery man had just dropped something off at the door. And, boy, did Frizzie ever love tattling on the family's dog. Every time Rocket would chew up something, Frizzie would meow until she got Mom's attention.

Maybe it's time to be more like Frizzie. Whenever you're feeling worried or afraid, go straight to your Master. He's right there. Unlike an oblivious pet owner, the

Lord actually knows why you're troubled. He's also got an answer to your problems, even before you ask. (But He loves it when you ask.)

Think about how much you love it when those under your care come to you with their concerns. It feels good, doesn't it? Can you imagine how much it blesses the Lord when you approach Him—not just in rough seasons, but blissful ones as well? He loves hanging out with His kids and isn't ruled by the clock. 24/7, He wants you to come to Him.

Lord, I'm sorry for the times I've run to others and not to You. I want to bring every worry, every concern, every joy, and every blessing straight back to You, the Giver of all blessings! How I praise You for making Yourself accessible to me, no matter the time of day or night.

AMEN.

44

Faithful Kitty

*Two are better than one, because they have a
good reward for their toil. For if they fall, one will lift
up his fellow. But woe to him who is alone when he
falls and has not another to lift him up!*

ECCLESIASTES 4:9–10 ESV

• • •

Monty knew the neighborhood well. He'd lived here all
his life, after all. His owner didn't mind if Monty roamed
a bit—in fact, he often put him outside for hours on
end. And boy, did Monty ever love to travel. He crossed
over the back fence into the neighbor's yard and ate the
dachshund's dog food. From there, he traveled to the
house across the street, where the nice lady always left
him a bowl of milk. After that, he would head up the
block to that one house where they always left the lid off
the trash can. Talk about hidden treasures!

Monty would eventually head home, belly full, and
his owner, Tina, would greet him with a smile. "How's
Mommy's little baby? Are you hungry, sweetie?" Then
she would fill his food bowl and he'd lap it up as if he
hadn't spent the whole day gorging.

Monty wasn't terribly faithful to his owner, was he?

Truth be told, he was even a little deceptive. Some would say he played her like a violin.

God created you to be faithful—to Him and to each other. This is true in marriages, of course, but there's a certain level of faithfulness that needs to take place between parents and kids, friends, and even coworkers.

Perhaps this is one reason God created us to live in community. He placed us in families, in neighborhoods, in churches, and so on. And He loves it when we stick together! There's power in numbers, after all. This is particularly important in the body of Christ. Think of how many people we can reach if we all work as a team.

It's tempting to wander like Monty, for sure. Roaming the neighborhood can be fun. But you know what's even more fun? Lifelong friendships and relationships with those you cherish. There's no greater gift you can give your loved ones than your faithfulness.

Lord, I will stick close to my people.
They've got my back and I've got theirs.
Together, we are a force to be reckoned with!
Thanks for my community, Father.

AMEN.

45

up the Down Stairs

"I have the right to do anything," you say—but not everything is beneficial. "I have the right to do anything"— but I will not be mastered by anything.

I CORINTHIANS 6:12 NIV

. . .

Ginger had never lived in a two-story before, so when her owner, Nancy, moved into a townhouse, the cat was intrigued. She had always loved heights. The up-and-down movement came naturally to her. But this stair situation seemed almost too good to be true! Had this special obstacle course been designed with her in mind, perhaps?

Day after day she tore up and down the stairs. She would race to the top, only to turn around and bound to the bottom, where the game would start all over again. Many times over, Nancy nearly lost her balance walking up or down the stairs because Ginger would come racing between her legs and almost knock her over. Thank goodness she never fell.

After a while, the constant up-and-down motion nearly wore Nancy out. She purchased a contraption that she called a baby gate. Ginger didn't like it one bit. It didn't take her long to learn how to jump over it, though.

Maybe you feel a bit like Ginger. Have you ever wanted something so badly that you were willing to jump over walls for it? Maybe it was a job or a promotion that you thought would make all the difference. Or was it a relationship you would do anything to fix, or a bad habit you just couldn't quit. Whatever it may have been, you just knew that if you achieved it, or could get your hands on it, then all your problems would disappear. How did that work for you?

The truth is the only thing, person, or place in this world that can bring true peace, hope, and stability, is Jesus. Are you running after Him with the same passion and intensity as you're running after what you want? And is what you want aligned with what God wants? Maybe it's time to stop running up and down the stairs and ask God about His plans for your life. Because when He is in control, He will do more with your life than you could ever possibly imagine.

Lord, i give all my wants and desires to you. Help me to stop doing things and running toward opportunities that don't align with your will for my life. i give it all to you.

AMEN.

46

Killing Time

*Making the best use of the time, because the
days are evil. Therefore do not be foolish, but
understand what the will of the Lord is.*

EPHESIANS 5:16–17 ESV

. . .

At the ripe old age of thirteen, Gizmo didn't have much
to do with his time but kill it. With his owner at work all
day, he spent hours resting on the back of the sofa or
chasing shadows on the floor. It's a good thing his owner
never asked, "What did you accomplish with your day?"
because Gizmo wouldn't have been able to come up
with a good answer.

When you're a cat, it's okay to waste the day away.
You can lounge in the sun, eat whenever you like, or play
with toys from sunup till sundown with no consequences.
For humans, though, whiling away the hours can prove
to be deadly.

Let's face it: it's hard to keep everything balanced.
When you're trying to handle work, family, and play,
things are often left undone. Sometimes it's easier to just
forget about it.

Here's a hard reality: When you continue pushing

things off, there are inevitable consequences. A messy kitchen can morph into a hazard zone if you're not careful. And bills that go unpaid can lead to utilities being shut off.

If someone asked the question "So, what did you get done today?" would you have an adequate answer? If so, great! If not—if too many hours were wasted on things that won't propel your life forward—it might be time to rethink your daily schedule.

Of course, the Sabbath is meant for resting. (Hey, even God took one day off!) But lounging around day after day, not getting things done? That's not a Sabbath rest. When you allow laziness to kick in—to the point of unreasonableness—you have to ask yourself if you are using the gifts He's provided you to do the work you are here for.

Lord, I need to learn how to balance my work, play, and rest. Help me find balance in my schedule, I pray.

AMEN.

47

Hair Balls

It is for freedom that Christ has set us free.
Stand firm, then, and do not let yourselves be
burdened again by a yoke of slavery.

GALATIANS 5:1 NIV

• • •

Ginny's cat, Shadow, was an incessant licker. Being a long-haired cat only complicated the situation. He would lie in the sunshine for hours a day, cleaning himself. The obsessive feline left loose hairs all over the house, which Ginny had to sweep up. Many times, Shadow would end up with a mouthful of hair and start gagging. More than once, Ginny thought she might lose him when he couldn't catch his breath. That's how bad the episodes got.

Still, Shadow refused to give up cleaning himself. He'd rather contend with the hair balls than do away with his obsessive habit. Perhaps he felt the reward outweighed the risk. Or maybe he just didn't stop to think about it at all.

Likely, you know the feeling of having something stuck in your throat, so you can sympathize with Shadow's predicament. When that happens, you can't figure out how to get it dislodged. So, you panic and think you're not going to make it. Then, miraculously, you manage to cough it up. Crisis averted!

Being caught up in our own selfishness can cause us to live with anger and bitterness, which is a bit like having a hair ball stuck in your throat. You want to get rid of it, but you seem to be trapped. So, you decide to live with it. Only, that doesn't work either. In the end you just want to throw your hands up in the air in defeat.

Don't give up. God will help you overcome if you'll just hand over the reins. Doing so means you can't keep running back to your selfish ways, though. Unlike that cat, you'll have to break that nasty habit. And habits are funny things. They like to stick around. You'll have no choice but to tell them to go in Jesus' name!

Lord, I'm so sorry I've clung to my bad habits. I want to break them, Father, but I'll need Your help! I'm reaching out to You today, handing off the reins.

AMEN.

48

Living Water

But whoever drinks of the water that I will give him will never be thirsty again. The water that I will give him will become in him a spring of water welling up to eternal life.

JOHN 4:14 ESV

. . .

Dixie had an annoying habit. In spite of the fact that she had a perfectly good water bowl, this peculiar feline chose to drink from the toilet in the downstairs bathroom. Many times over, her owner, Lynn, caught her in the act. Each time, she scolded her and closed the bathroom door. Still, at every available opportunity— say, one of the kids left the door cracked open just a smidgen—Dixie would sneak back in for a few sips of her favorite beverage. Sounds nasty, right? Why crave the tainted when she had pure, clean water at her disposal?

If we take a look at our own behaviors, we would have to admit that we're a lot like Dixie at times. Oh, we don't sip from the toilet, but we often head to tainted waters instead of lapping up the living water that Jesus provides. We are tempted by things that look bet- ter—relationships with the wrong people, activities with friends that compromise our beliefs, excessive use of alcohol, and so on. When we do this, we're sipping from other streams that were never meant for us. They're not satisfying or life-giving. They leave us thirsting for more.

Why would you ever trade out perfection for something bitter and unhealthy? The living water that Jesus offers includes an eternal payoff—eternity in heaven with Him. How could you ever top that?

It's time to get back to the living water today, girl! You'll never find anything as refreshing or life-giving. Spend time at the brook with your Savior. Watch as He tenderly cares for you and gives you all you need. His well is one that truly never runs dry.

Jesus, thank You for being the living water. I have all I need in You—salvation, wholeness, healing, and total satisfaction.

AMEN.

WHAT GREATER GIFT
THAN THE LOVE OF A CAT.

Charles Dickens

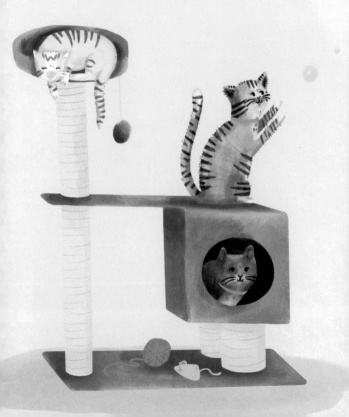

49

Furr-midable

*Be strong and courageous. Do not fear or be in
dread of them, for it is the LORD your God who goes
with you. He will not leave you or forsake you.*

DEUTERONOMY 31:6 ESV

. . .

Max, a Maine coon, wasn't just a big cat, though his size
did impress those he came in contact with. This big fellow also happened to be stronger than most other cats.
If he needed something under the chair, he somehow
managed to move the chair. If he wanted to pry the
pantry door open, he somehow managed to do it. If he
needed to fight off a rat or the occasional alley cat, no
problem. It seemed almost anything Max put his mind
to, he could do. His courage was admirable.

Maybe you know a few people like that. There are
plenty of powerhouses in your life, folks you admire. You
look up to them for a variety of reasons, but you're mostly
drawn to their bold faith. Everything they touch turns to
gold, or so it seems. Things—even hard things—seem
to resolve quicker for them. Their prayers get answered
with ease. Their adventures with God seem bigger,
bolder. Their faith seems huge in comparison to yours.

Here's the truth: all believers are powerhouses because every single child of God has the Holy Spirit residing inside of her. You carry just as much power inside of you as that spiritual giant you're admiring. It's true! You've got the same possibilities, the same potential outcomes, and the same penchant toward the miraculous. Why? Because the power you're craving doesn't come from you (and isn't dependent on you). It's all Him, sister!

Begin to see yourself as you are. You're a Maine coon, big and furr-midable, ready to do battle with the enemy of your soul. Hold that head high and march forward with the realization that God—the Almighty Creator of all—is working through you.

I'm so glad everything doesn't depend on me, Lord! Today I submit myself to Your Spirit's work inside of me. I'll be a willing vessel, Father. Use me for Your glory.

AMEN.

50

A Leap of Faith

And without faith it is impossible to please him,
for whoever would draw near to God must believe that
he exists and that he rewards those who seek him.

HEBREWS 11:6 ESV

• • •

Carla could hardly believe her eyes when she saw her cat, Jasmine, on the roof, perched as if ready for takeoff. The determined feline was pointed at the neighbor's roof, more than six feet away. But Carla couldn't fathom how the cat could make such a massive leap of faith without doing great harm to herself in the attempt.

She called out to Jasmine to stop her before she made a foolhardy mistake, but before she could get the words out, the cat shot through the air like a speeding bullet, body splayed. When she landed with ease on the neighbor's roof, Carla breathed a sigh of relief. Still, she wanted to chasten the feisty little thing. Whatever possessed the cat to think she could manage something that looked completely impossible from Carla's point of view?

There will be many times in life when you'll be asked to take a leap of faith, not unlike the leap that Jasmine made. Your perspective from up on the roof will be different from the point of view your friends and loved ones will have from down below. They might not get it. They might even think you're being foolish or impulsive. But if God has placed a belief for the impossible in your heart, keep on believing, keep on trusting, keep on hoping. Brace yourself, just as Jasmine perched herself in a take-off position. (Talk about a faith posture!)

What impossible thing are you believing for today? God wants to bolster your faith, even now, to make you into a woman who believes for the impossible. Get ready. It's coming! Oh, the places you will go and the things you will do with your hand in His!

Lord, there are big faith leaps coming.
I can feel it! Embolden me. Increase my faith.
Give me courage to leap when You say leap
and to trust that You will carry me all
the way. I'm looking forward to our
adventures together, Father!

AMEN.

DaySpring

LIVE YOUR FAITH

Dear Friend,

This book was prayerfully crafted with you, the reader, in mind. Every word, every sentence, every page was thoughtfully written, designed, and packaged to encourage you—right where you are this very moment. At DaySpring, our vision is to see every person experience the life-changing message of God's love. So, as we worked through rough drafts, design changes, edits, and details, we prayed for you to deeply experience His unfailing love, indescribable peace, and pure joy. It is our sincere hope that through these Truth-filled pages your heart will be blessed, knowing that God cares about you—your desires and disappointments, your challenges and dreams.

He knows. He cares. He loves you unconditionally.

BLESSINGS!
THE DAYSPRING BOOK TEAM

———